to Sharon:

Perplexity is the beginning of knowledge.

Gibran

hope you find as much use for it as I did.

Love,
Saphire

I CHING

THE BOOK OF CHANGES

TRANSLATED BY

FRANK J. MAC HOVEC, B.A., M.A.

———◆———

WITH ILLUSTRATIONS BY

MARIAN MORTON

The Peter Pauper Press

MOUNT VERNON, NEW YORK

INTRODUCTION

It was the Greek philosopher Heraclitus who said: "Nothing endures but change." That was 2,500 years ago. We are still in the midst of change—weather, seasons, people, technology. The I CHING, translated "book of changes," is devoted solely to the idea of change, and it was used in ancient China centuries before Heraclitus was born.

The I CHING consists of 64 hexagrams and their meanings. These were widely used in ancient China to foretell the future and to give practical advice. It supposedly contains every possible situation and so, in a way, it is an ancient Chinese guidebook in human relations.

Confucius so valued the I CHING that he called it "the perfect book" and he used it extensively in his university. Taoism was also influenced by it, evidenced by its heavy reliance on the balance of nature, opposites, and the importance of humility, sincerity, and moderation.

Most scholars agree that the I CHING is a product of the Classical Age of China (15th-3rd century B.C.). Its content probably dates back to the 11th century B.C., making it the oldest of the five classics of China and one of the world's oldest books.

Legend has it that the eight trigrams from which the 64 hexagrams evolved were discovered by Emperor Fu Hsi (c. 2800 B.C.) who observed them on the back of a tortoise. Fu Hsi is usually pictured with a tortoise at his feet. He is also said to have invented writing and devised a calendar.

Another legend credits King Wen (1231-1135 B.C.) with writing the book while imprisoned by Chou Hsin, last of the Shang dynasty. We know King Wen wrote summaries of the hexagrams and his son, Chou Kung (1211-1115 B.C.), first emperor of the Chou dynasty, wrote of the significance of each of the six lines of each hexagram.

How can you use this book? Read it as is and ponder its advice or as a kind of horoscope, a source of advice for the future, its original function. The ancients used tortoise shells and yarrow or milfoil stalks to determine, line by line, which hexagram applied to them. None of these methods is practical today. Some suggest tossing coins, but a simpler method is to shuffle prepared cards, each with a number from 1 to 64.

Select a card and the passage and hexagram of that number applies to the problem at hand. Or simply close your eyes, leaf through the book, and let your finger stop at random.

To follow the way of the ancients, always wrap the book in silk. Never rest it on any surface without its cover as a place mat or it will gradually lose potency. Store it high in the room, above standing shoulder height. Always face north, in the center of the room, when using the book. Prostrate yourself three times. The numbered cards and then the book itself are passed three times clockwise through rising incense smoke. Concentrate throughout on the day, event, or problem for which you seek guidance.

The object of this book is to provide you with the I CHING in simple modern English. English headings have been changed to better match the content of the passage. The passages themselves have been rephrased. It is hoped this version avoids the awkward 18th-19th century language and the deep scholarly analysis of other works, for such is not in keeping with the Chinese ideal of natural simplicity. But this introduction is too long! Spend your time in quiet contemplation of the timeless I CHING, not on the thoughts of unworthy writers who die and are forgotten. Let this be "the writer's hexagram" and number it, significantly, 0.

F. J. M.

I Ching: The Book of Changes

This concise handbook on human relations is from ancient China and may be the oldest book in the world.

I CHING

1. The Ch'ien Hexagram

THE STRENGTH OF THE DRAGON. Use this time to further develop your inner strength. Refrain from taking direct action. Be observant. Think carefully. Ponder, contemplate. Consult with those wiser and more knowledgeable than yourself. Avoid extremes. Develop quiet confidence. It is a time for solitude and serenity, time to quietly cultivate and develop the four noble attitudes of firmness, strength, moderation, and justice.

2. The K'un Hexagram

THE LOVING SERVICE OF THE EARTH MOTHER. Be perceptive. Avoid errors before they take place. Let your abilities flow naturally. Work with quiet efficiency. Exercise firm self-control in time of stress. Lead by following or appearing to follow. Achieve with just the right amount of effort. Let your work identify you and let it be a labor of love. Success comes through quiet efficiency, loving service, and conscientious devotion to duty.

3. The Chun Hexagram

GROWTH. Grow, move forward, with measured pace, checking yourself all along the way. Observe the situation closely and carefully, seeing all facets, all possible sources of trouble. Use firm but proper action where necessary. Delegate responsibility and accept help, but not so as to become dependent. Do not over-extend yourself. Be sure of yourself, sure of your ground, then move cautiously but surely ahead.

4. The Mêng Hexagram

LEARNING. From youth onward, life exerts continuing pressure on the individual. Guard your individuality lest the mind be unduly conditioned to conform. Accept those less experienced than you. Men, be respectful toward women. Develop virtues based on inner strength and signify them by outward self-restraint. Be yourself; do not emulate others. Do not be too forward, and discourage others from doing so. To do otherwise is foolish and ends in embarrassment. Effective learning, though, involves some unpleasant consequences. Be receptive and learning follows. Punishment is applied only to prevent future unreasonable extremes.

5. The Hsü Hexagram

WATCHFUL WAITING. Stop, look, and listen before you take action. Do one thing at a time or there is real danger. When faced with confusion, maintain self-control. When faced with a complex situation, realize it cannot be solved quickly or with one simple solution. Forget this and you slip into indecision, inviting your enemies to move in. Adapt to reality, stand by your convictions, but do not be unreasonable or antagonistic. Confusion is not constant. Use peaceful moments to compose yourself so your goal remains clearly in sight. No situation is hopeless. Be sensitive to help, accept it gratefully, and your situation improves.

6. The Sung Hexagram

CHALLENGE, CONFLICT. Do not take the initiative yourself, but join with others. If the situation is impossible, withdraw gracefully.

Live according to your means and work hard to merit your future without envying others. If you're wrong, being aggressive will not bring success. For inner peace and contentment, withdraw to yourself, to nature. Strive to be moderate, to "feel the balance" and you will do the right thing. The greater the number of problems, the more opportunity there is for growth. Enduring happiness means seeing the end to problems, the satisfaction of knowing effective solutions.

7. The Shih Hexagram

GROUP LEADERSHIP. Assuming your cause is just, planning is needed to achieve success. Respect the chain of command; assume those in authority earned and deserve the leadership role. The leader shares in the good and in the bad as one of the group. There is no victory without effective leadership; dissension and differences lead to defeat. Facing odds, withdraw gracefully and thus preserve maximum strength. Facing certain defeat, there is great need for strong leadership thus preserving group identity. Faced with success, share rewards wisely and unselfishly, to each according to his contribution, needs, and abilities, but beware of placing too much power in the wrong hands.

8. The Pi Hexagram

UNIFYING SPIRIT. Be genuine, sincere, like uncarved wood, real and natural. Be yourself. Preserve your integrity, dignity, and honor. Overextend yourself and you lose some of yourself. Be disloyal and you lose your honor. The wise accept those who look to them for help. They do not force themselves on others. They do not deceive nor do they unjustly criticize. They know that unity requires trust and mutual respect. Without these qualities there can be no unity. Without these qualities there can be no success.

9. The Hsiao Ch'u Hexagram

MODERATION. Move ahead, but as difficulties come, slow down, be less forceful and more thoughtful. By using moderation you avoid the constant stress which can wear you down and lessen your effectiveness. Rushing blindly ahead for a quick victory causes continual friction which saps energy. Be flexible, deftly maneuvering with the circumstances, constantly exploring alternatives and weighing the consequences. Stand by your colleagues with friendship and cooperation, for in unity there is great strength. Know that all things reach their peak, then wane. Success, too, comes by degrees, moderately, reaches a peak, and does not last forever.

10. The Lü Hexagram

TACT. Accept your position, however humble, and be content, for now, to be effective in it. Be simple, free, and uncomplicated. Use and

develop tact with moderation. Do otherwise and you will fail. Any goal, however unattainable it may seem, can be achieved by tact with moderation. Without this quality nothing is certain and failures are quite likely. Look back over your own life and you will see that success followed when this quality was put to effective use.

11. The T'ai Hexagram

PERSONAL DEVELOPMENT. Do not forget your friends as you succeed in life. Do everything in moderation. Retain your individuality and be realistic as you examine the situation, looking for new opportunities, accepting the risks within reason. You will change, for progress means change, change brought about by your dealing with situations and people. This should make you aware of your personal development. Be friendly to all, regardless of their position or relationship with you. Taking aggressive action may be appealing, but bad times will pass and being belligerent brings even more trouble than before. Accept what is inevitable; try as best you can to calm the situation. Regardless of how it looks to you, know that there is more good at work than evil.

12. The P'i Hexagram

FRUSTRATION. Undeserving people are succeeding and communication is difficult. Under these circumstances, it's best for you to withdraw and thus retain your integrity and individuality. Your friends will understand. Respect superiors for their position if not for their persons. But use your judgment, not theirs. You could succeed by cooperating with them, but if you do you will be ashamed of your own deceit. Do your duty where you are as long as you can and do not overstep your authority. Think about alternatives and prepare for any eventuality. No situation remains for long. Success is limited and happiness is short-lived.

13. The T'ung Jên Hexagram

FRIENDSHIP. Extend yourself in genuine friendship and not everyone responds to you in the same manner. There is a limit to friendship and this causes problems. Where there is distrust, there is alienation. Where there is alienation, there is deceit. Stand by your convictions and remain friendly. Others will see that you mean well and more clearly understand your opinions. In time, the relationship will deepen, earlier problems will be overcome, and friendship will develop. But realize that even this friendship has limits and will not become universal. Still, be happy that such progress is possible, for it is a step in the right direction.

14. The Ta Yu Hexagram

REAL WEALTH. Wealth has its mental as well as its physical aspects. Mental wealth is to feel unthreatened. It means you know the dangers of physical wealth and you restrain yourself accordingly. Your own thoughts and those of your friends will help you continue self-development despite affluence. Do good with your physical wealth, do not use it only for yourself. Keep your passions in due bounds, be respectful of the law, benevolent toward people, and do all this with sincerity and humility. Do otherwise and people react badly toward you and you will find yourself alone with only your physical wealth.

15. The Ch'ien Hexagram

HUMILITY. Be humble, not aggressive, and there will be little resistance to your aims. Humility is a virtue which you should continually develop. It means you realize that recognition and honors reward your ability but you continue as before. It means you respect superiors and appreciate those who work with and for

you. It means that in victory you are consider-
ate to those in the enemy camp. It means that
in defeat you exert self-discipline and cease
being aggressive. It means that in any and every
situation you lead by example.

16. The Yü Hexagram

HAPPINESS. Be tranquil and serene, perceptive to the slightest change and ready for immediate action. Be very careful about the
tendency in you to be dependent on others, to
indulge in pleasures, and to pursue affluence.
Foster cooperation and happiness in others by
being yourself, sincere and accepting. People
will respond well to this. Progress with the
many problems of everyday life should bring
satisfaction and spur you on to greater achieve-
ments. Indulging in an occasional treat, if kept
within reason, will add to your happiness, but
don't let it distract you unduly or become a
goal in itself.

17. The Sui Hexagram

ASSOCIATING WITH OTHERS. Remain true to yourself even though your goals may change. Do not hesitate to associate with those who disagree with you as well as with those with whom you agree. Associate, too, with those less experienced in preference to those more knowledgeable. Meet with better people; avoid the shallow and artificial. Deceitful people will approach you and you have a tendency to depend on them for the rewards they can bring. Rise above this. Preserve your integrity. Let excellence be your goal. Excellence and integrity are qualities which bring success and endure long after you have left the scene.

18. The Ku Hexagram

OVERCOMING BACKWARDNESS. Solve minor problems now while the solutions are still simple. There are consequences to any major change and you should know and understand them. Honor your parents even though you may disagree with them. Strengthen your position gradually. Move with deliberate speed, but not too quickly or there will be confusion. It is wrong to tolerate backwardness. With help you can reverse the cycle and your efforts will be appreciated. Remain somewhat aloof from the world and quietly improve yourself. In this way you will make of yourself something which will endure.

19. The Lin Hexagram

MOVING AHEAD. Do what is right despite the opinions of others and you will move ahead. Know that those who do not clearly see the right follow those who do. When power comes to you do not be careless with it but remain perceptive and thoughtful or trouble follows. You will succeed by doing right, having right thoughts, and associating with people who do

the same. When you lead, seek out those who are able and give them a free hand. Help those who come to you; they will improve with your assistance.

20. The Kuan Hexagram

PERCEPTION. Your perception is faulty. You have a tendency to miss the point, to lose sight of the dynamics of the situation, of what's really happening. For others this may not be too serious, but you should know better. You will succeed only if you closely examine the situation, see what's really there, and plan effective action accordingly. People with good judgment and objective perception succeed. When you succeed, help others in your new position. This will help you even more. Be realistic and take a good look at yourself, not so much as an individual who stands alone, but as a person who reacts to and with others. Knowing how and where you fit into society and life is the object.

21. The Shih Ho Hexagram

ACCEPTING PUNISHMENT. When you are punished, realize that the punishment was just. The more serious the offense, the greater the punishment. You will still feel humiliated even though you were guilty and justice was served. This is understandable. Daily living is complex and everyone makes mistakes. Resolve to do better, to grow from the experience. If you had been treated leniently would you have learned anything? If you were judge, would you have been as objective and impartial? React emotionally and evil will grow within you out of all realistic proportion and guilt feelings will continue unabated.

22. The Pi Hexagram

THE ARTIFICIAL YOU. Resist the tendency to appear what you are not, a false front. Be yourself. Resist the tendency to enjoy material things for their own sake. Enjoy life instead. Resist the tendency to rest on your previous successes, to take yourself and others for granted. Continue growing. You will have to choose between material and non-material growth. Know that there are limits to material growth but there are no limits to inner enlightenment. With inner enlightenment you can be a friend to everyone. You can then become what you should be, and know the whole truth of human relationships.

23. The Po Hexagram

DEALING WITH DECEIT. Beware of deceitful people who undermine organizations, damage character, and spread evil rumors and ill feeling. Be honest and sincere with them but do not use their methods. It may seem that these people succeed and there is no way to stop them. It will take courage, perseverance, and renewed dedication to better principles. You also need all the help you can get from able people you can trust. There is no easy way out of this situation. You will get little support and the situation will seem hopeless. The negative forces will weaken, however, influenced by what is right and good. Know that evil carries within itself the means of its own destruction. Remain on the side of truth and right and you cannot be destroyed.

24. The Fu Hexagram

MINOR SETBACK. You will have a minor setback, but suffer no great loss. Regain your balance and continue on. Your recovery will be quicker if you have developed good self-control. Emulating someone you admire also helps. You have a tendency to do what is practical rather than what is right, to seek immediate gain and forget about the long run. No great harm comes of this but it isn't good for you. You can associate with strangers, but it is your friends who help you be yourself. Realize your shortcomings; don't make excuses. Plunge recklessly ahead and you are in danger of sustaining a great loss.

25. The Wu Wang Hexagram

CHILDLIKE SIMPLICITY. A childlike simplicity is a virtue which should be developed. It means doing what is right, because it is right, not for any selfish reason. Material wealth will come anyway. There will be misfortune, but no serious harm. The real, natural you is resilient and strong. Be your natural self and you can do no harm. When misfortune comes, let nature take its course. The situation improves by itself, without the need for any action on your part. Accept reality, whatever fate brings. Oppose this and you stand alone.

26. The Ta Ch'u Hexagram

SELF CONTROL. You face very real problems. Get hold of yourself. You think the odds are against you. Do not act too quickly. Quietly gather yourself together and accumulate inner strength. Help will come from others facing the same problems. Danger remains even though the problems fade away. Remain alert and perceptive. When confronted with great force, disperse it with quick remedies and unique preventive measures. Understanding the source of the problem will enable you to control it. Eliminate problems in this way and move ahead.

27. The I Hexagram

SELF-SUFFICIENCY. You have a tendency to be selfish, to envy others, to unjustly use others. Nothing good can come from this attitude. There is a great need for able people. Know your strengths and weaknesses and follow the advice and example of one you respect and admire. Realize you cannot succeed alone. Do not hesitate to teach others what you know to be true. Understanding enables you to succeed against odds, thus helping yourself and others.

28. The Ta Kuo Hexagram

CONTINUING PROBLEMS. Start with a careful study of important issues. Your spirit will be renewed. If necessary, associate with lesser people to gain insight. Beware of the tendency to be over-confident, to move too quickly, against advice. To do so means more trouble, making the situation more difficult. Rely on your own inner strength and that of others. Do not trust only in those above you, ignoring others, or you will sink deeper into trouble. Do what is right regardless. Trouble will seem to continue, but realize that being right is reward enough and is best for you in the long run.

29. The K'an Hexagram

SHORTCOMINGS INCREASE PROBLEMS. If the situation seems hopeless, it is because you have become accustomed to the wrong way of

doing things. You are lost. The more you try, the more lost you become. Realize you can't solve problems all at once, but rather by degrees, through creative solutions. Do not take action until the solution makes itself obvious. Do otherwise and problems become more complicated. Be honest, sincere, and direct. No need for flattery, subtle intrigue, or gifts of tribute. Allow ambition to drive you too hard and troubles remain as before. Rather, exert just enough pressure to overcome obstacles. Do not overdo it. If you allow your shortcomings to predominate, you will surely fail.

30. The Li Hexagram

THE GOLDEN MEAN. The many little frills surrounding a situation confuse you. Look for the central theme, the source, the seed idea, and the solution is easier. Be reasonable. As you grow older you see that life is very fragile. This causes depression. Do not over-react to cure the sadness. To do so is unnatural, not the real you. And as you grow older you see that human nature is vain. This causes cynicism. Re-examine and rededicate yourself to your motives and values. The lesson here is not to be misled by the myriad parts of a problem, but rather to seek out its central theme, its source, its seed idea, and avoid extremes and excess.

31. The Hsien Hexagram

INFLUENCING OTHERS. There is an influencing force at work which is not obvious to you. You, too, exert influence of which you are not fully aware. You cannot influence others by being submissive, by ingratiation, or through sentimentality. It doesn't last. If you lack self-discipline you will be distracted by extraneous details and your influence is therefore dissipated. Try to influence someone when you are not sure of yourself and when you lack confidence and you will not be effective. And if your goal is not important, your influence will be minimal. And if you use only talk to influence others, results will also be minimal.

32. The Hêng Hexagram

MATURITY. To endure, you must be mature. It is not mature to act impulsively or with thoughtless force. Maintain self-control. Be yourself. Otherwise trouble comes from every direction. And good intentions are not enough. Neither are custom and tradition. They help, but to be mature means using good judgment, doing the right thing at the right time. This is especially difficult if you hold high office, because the many pressures of office becloud your vision, sap energy, and cause you continual anxiety.

33. The Tun Hexagram

STRATEGIC WITHDRAWAL. You are in a situation much like fighting a rear-guard action, the last to have contact with the enemy. Withdraw quietly and gracefully. There isn't much choice. To further confuse the matter, there seems to be many experts on the scene. The ideal is to use these experts but to see they don't get in the way. Withdraw accepting the reality of the situation, preserving your strength and self-identity, holding firmly to your convictions. Lesser people cannot do this. Timing is vitally important. Move according to careful plan, at just the right time, prepared for any eventuality. To do so requires thorough study of the situation. The need for withdrawal must be so obvious there can be no doubt as to its need.

34. The Ta Chuang Hexagram

OPTIMAL INFLUENCE. Your position is less than you wish despite your abilities. Your enthusiasm exceeds the needs of your present position. Do not be impatient and force your hand. It won't work. In time opportunity will come. Use your enthusiasm now to further de-

velop your strengths and abilities, thus preparing yourself for a better future. If there is trouble, using too much force will bring misfortune. Feel the balance, be moderate and patient, and success will come. Do not lapse into indifference and let your energy wane. Realize your situation but do not lash out. To do so will surely make the situation worse.

35. The Chin Hexagram

SUCCEEDING. Remain calm when you are passed over for advancement. When you are advanced, it will seem to you that you are unable to communicate effectively with your superiors. Do what is right and you will be rewarded. Move forward and you will get support. Try to take unfair advantage and you will be discovered and exposed. As you succeed, continue with self-discipline and self-restraint. Don't look back with regret at disappoinments and failures. Punish wrongdoing but be careful when doing so to strangers.

38

36. The Ming I Hexagram

BEING MISUNDERSTOOD. Try to improve yourself and you are criticized and ridiculed. Be true to yourself despite being misunderstood. It is painful but not fatal. Remain steadfast and gradually you grow ever stronger. Your time will come and with it ultimate victory. When you have won, do but do not overdo. With patient moderation the most deeply rooted problems are overcome. When you are at the heart of the problem it might be wise to withdraw, preserving your strength and holding firmly to your principles. This requires courage and sharp perception. When all is darkness you have a tendency to overlook sources of help and also to unwittingly ignore your own sense of duty.

37. The Chia Jên Hexagram

THE FAMILY. There are definite rules for the home. Be too permissive with children and there will be trouble with them later. The wife should perform her duties with quiet devotion, thus ensuring the well-being of the family. The government should do the same for the nation. Permissiveness and strictness must be kept in balance, but it is better to err on the side of being too strict than being too permissive. The wife should efficiently manage the household budget, thus ensuring the welfare of the family. The government should do the same for the nation. The husband should rule with firmness, strength, moderation, and justice, thus preserving the peace and unity of the family. And the government should do the same for the nation.

38. The K'uei Hexagram

ALIENATION. When in a crisis, under pressure, you make mistakes. If someone deserts the group, do not seek after him, but let him return by himself. If someone infiltrates the group, tolerate him, and he will leave by himself. Misunderstanding and poor communication separate people. Friendly, informal chats overcome this and are more effective than formal meetings. When the situation looks hopeless, that is the time to stand by your convictions, true to yourself above all else. Do this and it will end well. Find a fellow-spirit in the enemy camp and, together, attain the goal. Deeper friendship will grow between you and misunderstanding will cease.

39. The Chien Hexagram

OVERCOMING OBSTACLES. You will meet with a serious obstacle. Wait for just the right moment to take action. Carefully study the situation and choose the optimal solution in keeping with your convictions and abilities. Sometimes it is best to withdraw, thus preserving your strength. Sometimes it is best to join with others, thus being stronger as a group. Sometimes it is best to singlehandedly attack, thus attracting allies to your side. Sometimes it is best to do nothing, thus knowingly choosing the defensive role.

40. The Chieh Hexagram

LIBERATION. When there seem to be no obstacles in your path, pause for a moment. With patient moderation, gradually and meticulously eliminate negative influences and thus improve and strengthen your position. New friends will be better for you. Avoid the tendency to become lost in the spoils of victory. Avoid this so as to achieve greater success in the future. You need to renew your spirit, regain your bearings. Others may disagree, but they will see that this is right for you. You will gain new insight, renewed strength, and you will be able to overcome any obstacle.

41. The Sun Hexagram

SELFLESSNESS. Help superiors, provided your help is well received and no harm can come from it. Serve loyally but not to your own detriment and not if it is undignified or dishonest. Two can have a close relationship, but with three such closeness is not possible because of rivalry and dissimilar interests. Like interests make for a closer relationship. Free yourself of bad habits and new and better friendships will result. Success will come, with fewer and fewer obstacles, and with less anxiety. Your power and influence will increase and you can dispense them without fear of their waning. Others will see how genuine and unselfish you are and join with you.

42. The I Hexagram

INSPIRATION. Your help comes from above. Use it well. Forget previous misfortune. You succeed because your goodness matches and blends with eternal goodness. Learn from your mistakes. When asked to mediate differences, be moderate and just and you will be trusted. Do what is right with firmness because it is right, without ulterior motive. If you fail you may lose the trust and confidence of others. If you fail it will be because you did not perceive the situation well, and you acted too quickly.

43. The Kuai Hexagram

```
━━━━━━━━━━
━━━━━━━━━━
━━━━━━━━━━
━━━━━━━━━━
━━━━━━━━━━
━━━━  ━━━━
```

REMAIN STEADFAST. Act too quickly, without a good plan, without sufficient thought, and you will make mistakes. Be alert, perceptive, and no evil can befall you. Take a firm stand, openly, but not too aggressively — the time is not right for it. Be courteous, not antagonistic. You may be misunderstood at first, but this will pass. Resist the wish to use excessive force. When provoked, you tend to lose control. You must be dedicated if you hope to overcome major obstacles. Success is within reach but you cannot achieve it alone. The same problem you now face will appear again in the future.

44. The Kou Hexagram

```
━━━━━━━━━━
━━━━━━━━━━
━━━━━━━━━━
━━━━━━━━━━
━━━━━━━━━━
━━━━  ━━━━
```

NEGATIVE INFLUENCES. There is a person of negative influence on the scene. Unless controlled, this will cause more trouble. Pre-

vent the spread of this influence but avoid excessive force. Use kindly moderation. You will consider joining with the opposition, a most serious situation requiring great insight. But conditions will prevent this. Because you don't associate with the majority, they will not support you. Be tolerant and benevolent to those below you. Do not brag or preach to them. Because you criticize you will be criticized, a challenge to your self-control, but continue to speak the truth and it will have a good effect.

45. The Ts'ui Hexagram

UNIFYING SPIRIT. You should join with others in a unifying spirit. Seek help and you will get it. You will then think more clearly and be happy. There is a force beyond your knowledge which is drawing you and others together. Do not resist it. Good fortune will result. There is no need for pretense or formality between friends. If some stand in your way, go to someone in the center, ally yourself to him

and follow him. There will be some embarrassment but it will pass. You will be accepted and
entrusted with leadership. You will have good
fortune without seeking it. Not everyone un-
derstands you and some use you for your influence. Continue doing right and these negative factors fade away. You will ally yourself
with one who misjudges you. Saddened by this
but resolute, the unifying spirit which you have
helped build will endure.

46. The Shêng Hexagram

ONWARD AND UPWARD. There is no obstacle in your path. You are warmly received
and your ability, sincerity, and loyalties are
obvious. Because there is no resistance, you
tend to be overly aggressive. Your success has
a spiritual and temporal aspect, coming from
above and through the help of friends. Superiors trust you and will reward you. Do not
let all this lull you into carelessness and indifference. Proceed carefully and thoughtfully.

47

You will succeed if you are careful, but move blindly ahead and nothing will go right.

47. The K'un Hexagram

OUT OF DARKNESS. You are not too alert, not perceptive enough, and you will suffer for it. Problems, unforeseen because of your lack of vision, will multiply and confuse you. Everyday problems disturb you. Even when there is some improvement, you remain depressed. You will be helped by someone in authority who seeks your guidance. Find yourself through quiet contemplation. Confusion will continue, you will be over-sensitive, and you will trust in the wrong things. If in a responsible position, help those under you. This may be difficult because of your status. Good intentions will produce good results. There will be obstacles above and below you but the situation will improve. Maintain self-control. Don't let it wear you down. Get hold of yourself, realize your mistakes and your shortcomings, and the improvement will continue.

48. The Ching Hexagram

FIRST THINGS. You are surrounded by negative influences and you are very much alone. It is because you have neglected your better self and you are wasting your abilities. Your good qualities are not being used, overlooked by your superiors. Your friends look upon this with regret. For a time you will be ineffective, but stop anyway and get a firm grip on yourself. It is worth it. Only the relaxed, natural leader helps and inspires others, really contributes, and is respected and admired for it.

49. The Ko Hexagram

TIMELY CHANGE. You are frustrated, but resist the urge to strike back. Wait for the opportune time, then take firm and decisive action. But only after careful thought and when you have the support of others. Resist the urge to be overly aggressive. Even so, some will complain that you overdid it. In time they will understand. You succeed because of high ideals, inner strength, and the moderate use of power. People will see that these are good qualities and support you. When you have achieved major goals, follow through to minor ones, thus completing the cycle of success.

50. The Ting Hexagram

HIGH IDEAS. As negative influences diminish you are able to continue toward your goal. You will be envied for your success, but continue on despite this. In time you will confront problems which overshadow your ability. You will have high ideas but they will be impractical. You will try to do great things when you are not able. You will seek more responsibility with insufficient knowledge. You will fail and you will be embarrassed. Be humble and receptive and others will help you. Wisdom is yours if you but want it. By being gentle and sincere help will come from above, the source of all goodness.

51. The Chen Hexagram

THE WEB OF ANXIETY. Sudden events make you tense but this will pass. A major setback will cost you in material things but you will succeed in another way. In time you will regain what was lost. Anxiety grows from repeated misfortunes. Overcome this by meeting each situation with just enough force, always retaining self-control. Obstacles and problems will continue. Perceive the core of the problem and you can more easily overcome it. The key is moderation. Overdo it and problems deepen. Keep a distance from such a web of anxiety. Some will criticize you for it but you will be doing the right thing and you will save yourself from much unnecessary pain.

52. The Kên Hexagram

STOP, LOOK, AND LISTEN. Stop and take a good look at yourself and your situation. See

what is there, not what you want to see. Study and think about it. Do not be distracted. You cannot help what your superiors do, even if it is wrong, but you are responsible for what you do. Inactivity should not disturb you, for you can use the time to contemplate who and where you are. Be yourself, but rise above selfishness to achieve a selfless serenity. Choose words carefully, speak only when you have something to say, and speak meaningfully, thus avoiding embarrassment. Do these things and you will achieve union with the universe.

53. The Chien Hexagram

CONTINUED GROWTH. Because you are inexperienced your slow but sure progress will be ridiculed. This is painful but is part of effective learning. Self-confidence comes in time and your work will earn rewards, socially and materially. When you overdo it you create problems. The situation will worsen, presenting real danger, unless and until you realize your strengths and weaknesses and adjust to them. By being humble and receptive problems further diminish. Some deceitful people may stand in your way but you will ultimately triumph, reach your goal, and serve as a worthy example to others.

54. The Kuei Mei Hexagram

PASSIVE PROGRESS. Your superiors will trust in you. Choose to remain inconspicuous and work from within. Your dedication and ability will overcome weaknesses in the group. Be realistic: it is better to do some good indirectly in this way than to strive actively and accomplish nothing. Do not compromise your principles. Do not allow your ambition to dull your vision. Do not act only for the sake of appearances, but be genuine in thought and deed. Do this and you will make progress.

55. The Fêng Hexagram

USING AND ABUSING. Cooperate with a future leader and you will profit by it. Others will take advantage of this leader and get in your way. Do not take action about this or there will be distrust and resentment. Be sincere and genuine with this leader. These other people will get the attention of the leader and your effectiveness will diminish. Continue doing the best you can. The situation will improve and you will regain your influence. You will be promoted because of your loyalty and ability. But beware, for there is a strong tendency within you to let affluence spoil you, alienating you from your friends and even from your family.

56. The Lü Hexagram

RECKLESS AMBITION. You are not satisfied with your position and you believe in advancing regardless of the cost. This attitude will cause you trouble. Better to be humble and retain your integrity. You will advance, but in doing so you will become antagonistic and inconsiderate, and you will lose what you have gained. Inferior people have great ambitions and limited abilities. They are not comfortable because they are strangers unto themselves. You will succeed again and get the help of influential friends with good contacts. But again you will become antagonistic and inconsiderate.

57. The Sun Hexagram

SEARCH OUT EVIL. You are confused. Get a firm grip on yourself. You are being influenced by negative factors which are beyond your knowledge. Search them out, expose them, and they will fade away. You can overdo this by analyzing the same factors over and over, again and again, thus neutralizing yourself by inactivity from over-activity. Your successful victory over evil will gain respect and admiration.

Continue the good work, checking yourself before and after taking action. Your success may be hampered if you trace back too many problems for you will then find you do not have the power to eliminate all of them, your energy having been dissipated.

58. The Tui Hexagram

BALANCE AND PLEASURE. Because you are serene and content, material possessions and sensual pleasures tempt you. Preserve your dignity and honor. Submit to pleasure at this time and misfortune will follow. Anxiety is caused by the dilemma of having to judge how far to pursue pleasure. It is always better to seek higher pleasures, those which lead to the fully enlightened mind. Guard against the tendency to associate with lesser people who will use your abilities to evil ends. Know that it is often foolish pride which drives people to seek material things and selfish pleasures.

59. The Huan Hexagram

HUMAN TRUTH. There is little chance of misunderstanding where there is quick response to immediate needs. Be abusive and you alienate people. Be accepting and you attract people. Be moderate and you will have no regrets later. To help others, you must forget yourself. Knowing this is to be truly enlightened. Knowing this, one can rise above personal feelings. In time of crisis, such an attitude is the keystone of progress. Dangers are removed and peace endures.

60. The Chieh Hexagram

RULES. Realize the limits of your ability and do not proceed beyond them. It is time now to take action. Wait and it will be too late. Proceed according to careful plan and all is well. Ignore your plan and there is misfortune. Do not waste time and energy. Understand all sides of a situation and take just the right action at just the right time. Follow the same rules you expect others to follow and they will respect you for it. Overdo the rules and people rebel. Justice should be quick and firm. Even so, some evil will always remain.

61. The Chung Fu Hexagram

BE YOURSELF. It is time for thoughtful deliberation. You are stable, as ready to face and dispense with problems as you will ever be. If you engage in intrigue, anxiety will increase within you. State your case firmly and the good effect will spread. Depend on others for your moods and there is insecurity. Your feelings are not then your own and you are no longer your true self. Be humble and receptive and inspiration will come from above. Realize when it comes that it is for you alone to absorb and use. Be careful with words, for there is a limit to their effectiveness. Being natural, real, sincere, unifies all.

62. The Hsiao Kuo Hexagram

TIMING. Do not take action prematurely. You must be ready, seasoned, with mature judgment, if you are to succeed. Be cooperative, work with whomever is available. Because you ignore warning signs you will overlook dangerous situations and you will be hurt. Act in moderation. Use care and self-control. You cannot succeed without the help of others. And there is no one to help you. You search, but in vain. Eventually an experienced person will come to help you and success follows. You pay too much attention to minor details and in doing so cause trouble for yourself and for others.

63. The Chi Chi Hexagram

COMPLACENCY. You will complete your task just before you are overwhelmed by widespread confusion. Despite your best efforts, your superiors do not seem to confide in you. Be patient, remain loyal, do your best, and their trust will come. When victory comes, there is a need for effective leadership. Lesser men cannot control the situation. Having achieved victory, being pompous or belligerent invites misfortune. When all goes well, evils are easily overlooked. See that you are not so complacent. People see what they want to see, but what actually happens is because of the facts. Feelings are facts since they influence what happens.

64. The Wei Chi Hexagram

GREAT PROBLEMS, GREAT PLANS. You strive to make progress amid confusion. If the time is not right you will suffer a humiliating defeat. Control yourself, keep your strength ready. When the time for change comes you will not be able to succeed alone. Try and you will fail. The problem you face is a great one and it will influence the future. Great problems require great plans. Concentrate on immediate needs first. Be positive. Your attitude and sincerity will bring help from allies. Victory will come and a new and better future with it. Relax and rejoice, but in moderation. Excess forfeits all gains.